step-by-step
FREE-MOTION
QUILTING

Turn 9 Simple Shapes into 80+ Distinctive Designs

Best-selling author of
First Steps to Free-Motion Quilting

CHRISTINA CAMELI

stashBOOKS®

an imprint of C&T Publishing

Publisher: Amy Marson

Creative Director: Gailen Runge

Art Director / Book Designer:
Kristy Zacharias

Editor: Teresa Stroin

Cover Designer: April Mostek

Production Coordinators: Rue Flaherty
and Freesia Pearson Blizard

Production Editor: Alice Mace Nakanishi

Illustrator: Christina Cameli

Photography by Diane Pedersen,
unless otherwise noted

Photo Assistant: Mary Peyton Peppo

For Charlton Woods

Published by C&T Publishing, Inc., P.O. Box 1456, Lafayette, CA 94549

Library of Congress Cataloging-in-Publication Data

Cameli, Christina, 1976-

Step-by-step free-motion quilting : turn 9 simple shapes into 80+ distinctive designs / best-selling author of First steps to free-motion quilting, Christina Cameli.

pages cm

ISBN 978-1-61745-024-2 (soft cover)

1. Machine quilting--Patterns. 2. Patchwork--Patterns. 3. Patchwork quilts. I. Title.

TT835.C356173 2015

746.46--dc23

2014019946

Printed in China

10 9 8 7 6 5 4 3 2 1

Contents

Introduction

This book is the natural outcome of my appetite for new quilting designs, my passion for getting quilters to try new things, and my love of making complicated things simpler. I hope it thrills you. It certainly thrilled me to create it!

I've packed the book with quilting designs. They are fresh, easy-to-replicate designs that are perfect for beginner and intermediate free-motion quilters. Each design includes instructions for making it. But that's not what makes this book special.

The unique thing about this book is that the designs are all created from a small set of easily sketched shapes. Think circles, wavy lines, and loops—things you could doodle in a heartbeat. Combining and recombining this group of nine simple "elements" gave me hundreds of design possibilities. I've picked my favorites, from straightforward to striking, to share with you.

Working with simple shapes gives you a head start on the quilting design. Your mind already understands how the shapes are formed, so you just need a little practice putting them together. Thinking about quilting this way, even beginners can make beautiful and interesting designs. You don't have to know how to draw, you don't need experience, and you don't even need a fancy machine! I quilt on my domestic machine, and I've created these designs with the home machine quilter in mind.

If you want to try new things with your quilting, you just need a place to start. I hope the pages that follow give you that starting place. I want you to think, "That's a great design" and "I can do that!" Because you can.

Here's to making beautiful things happen.

Find Your Favorite Designs

The Elements

Following are the nine elements that together make up all the designs in this book. I've picked simple shapes that are easy to sketch. Keep in mind this idea of sketching. Free-motion quilting for most home quilters is more sketchy than precise. Don't stress.

CIRCLE

The circle is surely one of the most useful shapes in quilting. Circles have an attractive effect when quilted, and they are quite versatile for filling in space. Are your circles lopsided or oval sometimes? Mine too!

Occasionally you'll leave a circle open. Sometimes many circles will be joined together into pebbling or pebble lines. These types of designs are described further in Pebbling (page 21) and Traveling (page 18).

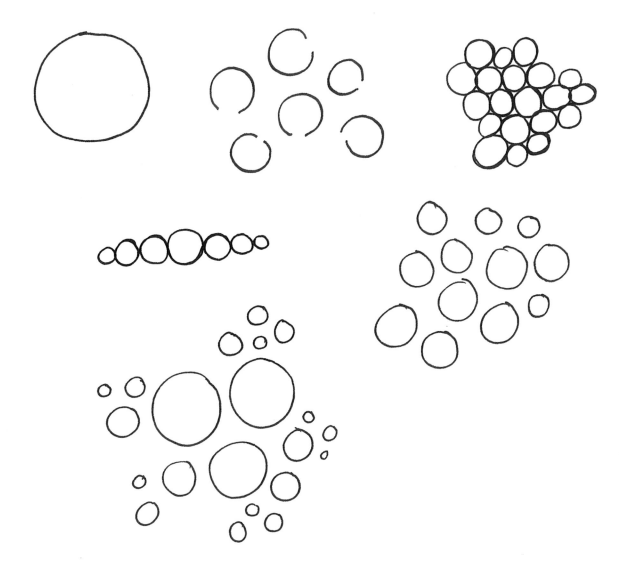

CURVING LINES

Lines with gentle curves provide great texture and frequently get us from one place to the next in our designs. These lines don't need to be precise or perfect. Just head in the direction you want to go and let your line wiggle as much or as little as you'd like.

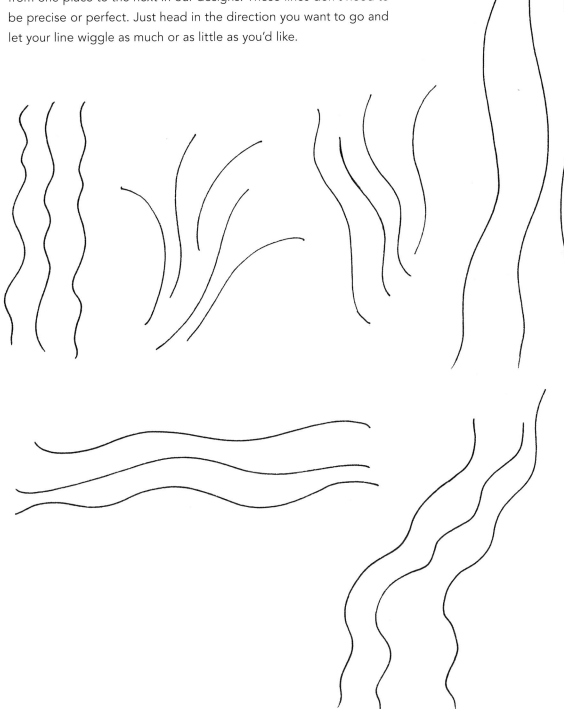

ℓ LOOP

Shaped like a cursive letter "e," loops are well loved by beginning quilters. They are sometimes tall, sometimes squat. You may string together several loops in a row.

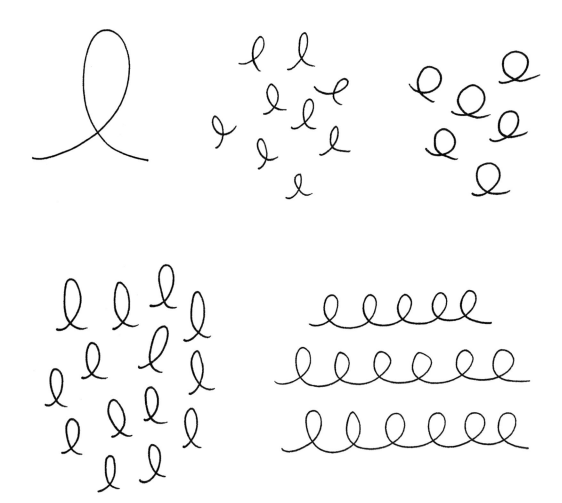

DROP

The drop shape is pointed at one end and curved at the other. It can be fat or skinny as needed. Sometimes the point of the drop will be left open. Sometimes a drop will bend to one side. Open drop shapes can be easily joined in a fan arrangement or a vertical column.

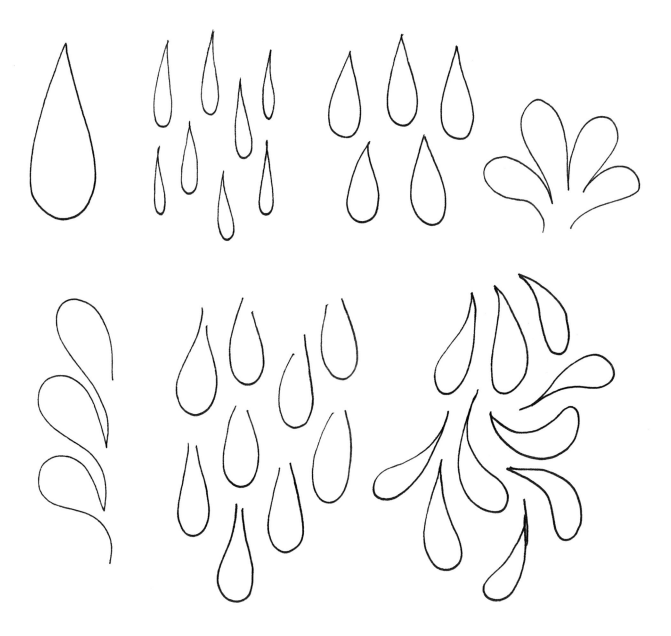

⟳ SPIRAL

Spirals can take on a lot of looks and are great space fillers. Most often you will make a path into the middle of a spiral, come to a point, and then work your way back out in the open space of the inward spiral path.

If you're filling a space with a spiral, the spiral should go right up against the first edge you pass. But make sure to leave room along the opposite edge (as well as between the spiral revolutions) to allow space to work back out of the spiral.

Spirals can be just a hint of a whirl or tightly wound, or made skinny by traveling back out along the original inward spiral path. You will often use spirals in rows.

Occasionally, your design will depend on exiting the spiral along the inside or the outside. In these illustrations, the blue line travels along the inside and the red line travels along the outside of the spiral.

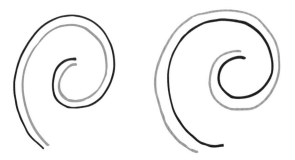

LEAF

At its simplest, the leaf design is two gentle curves that meet at a point. Occasionally you will keep the bottom ends of the curves apart to create an open leaf shape. Leaves are sometimes worked into flower shapes. Do remember that Mother Nature rarely makes her leaves exactly the same, so we needn't either.

Sometimes a gentle line up the middle of a leaf creates a center vein.

THE "S" CURVE

Unlike other curving lines, "S" curves have a regular, predictable undulation to them. They can still be imperfect; they just need to have a rhythmic back-and-forth pattern to make the designs work. Sometimes the "S" is dynamic and other times stretched out to just a hint of undulation. Sometimes "S" curves are mirrored to create a patterned effect.

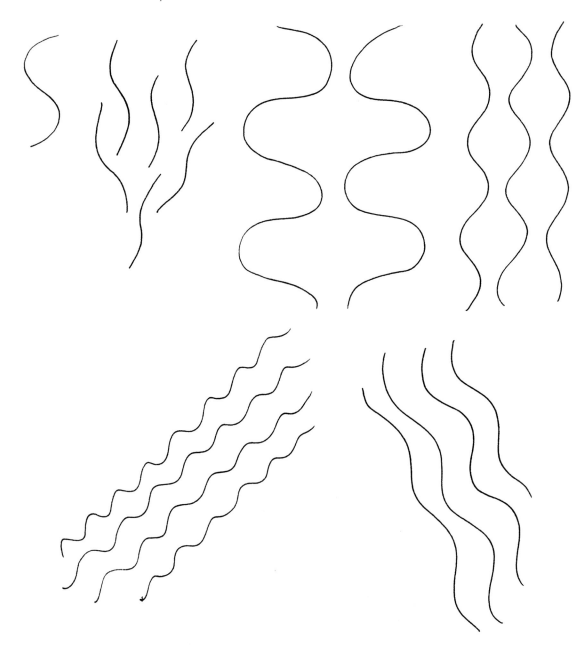

ARC

An arc is a simple curve that returns to the line or level that it started from. Arcs can be shallow, tall, or anywhere in between. Arcs are often used in a row or along a curved path.

GRASS

The grass shape is created with two wavy lines that meet at a point. The bottom of the shape can be open or closed. The two sides of the grass blade do not need to be symmetrical. Grass shapes can be arranged to create a flower, and open grass shapes can join together in a column.

Things to Know

ABOUT THIS BOOK

First things first: I'll use the word "motif" a lot. To be clear, a motif is an individual unit that we repeat to create the quilting design. Motifs are made up from the basic elements introduced in the first chapter. Some motifs are simple (FIGURE A), while others are complex. FIGURE B

Repeat a motif in a particular way and you have a design. Each design in this book includes instructions and drawings to explain how the individual motif is formed. I show completed steps in black and the current step in color. This should help you identify where the line travels over previous parts of the design. Dotted lines show the next step. Arrows are used to show the direction the line is taking. FIGURE C

Most of these designs will work well in small or large scale. You may choose to quilt a design smaller for a small piece like a pillow, or larger for finishing a quilt. Designs worked on a small scale will create dense, high-impact quilting and the quilting will take longer to finish. Designs worked larger will finish quicker, but you may have less of the play of light and shadow in the finished quilted texture. You may also find yourself limited by how large you can make certain elements. If your design has a large circle or drop shape, for instance, you may be limited by how large you are able to comfortably create these shapes with the space you have available under your machine arm. I strongly recommend practice stitching to help determine the scale you want to work your design.

Finally, as you will see, my sketches in this book are just that: sketches. I let them be imperfect, and the beauty of the pattern still comes forth. I hope you can give yourself the same freedom to embrace irregularities. To that end, I have purposely focused on organic designs with some unpredictability. When variation is expected in the design, the stitching can be successful without being executed perfectly. The leaves or circles might be varying sizes, the arcs might not all match up, and the lines might wobble, but even with these irregularities the design should still work.

A.

B.

C.

SKILLS FOR THE FREE-MOTION QUILTER

Traveling

The designs in this book are continuous-line designs. Working with a continuous line lets you quilt interesting designs without the impracticality of stopping and cutting your thread over and over. For many of the designs in this book, you will occasionally need to travel along an area you've already stitched to get to the next part of the design.

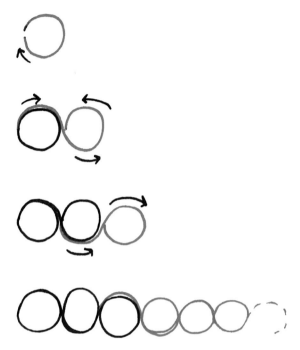

Here is the simplest example: a line of pebbles. You start by making one pebble. Then, to get to the other side of the pebble to start a new pebble, you travel halfway around the pebble along the circle you've already made. You continue that pattern, going one and a half times around each circle, to move in the direction you want.

With traveling you may not always hit the original line exactly. That's okay. When you step back from the quilting, these little inconsistencies will blend into your overall stitched pattern. Traveling is a skill, and, like all skills, it will take practice. If you're not happy with the quality of your traveling, choose designs that don't have much traveling.

Flexibility

Filling space evenly with a quilting design requires flexibility. Sometimes you'll need to make adjustments as you go to accommodate the space you have. You may make fewer petals than the motif calls for to fit in a tight space. You may add more leaves to keep your motif from finishing in the wrong spot. You may decide not to echo a motif because you're already in the right place to start the next one. Give yourself the freedom to adjust your design on the fly.

The specifics of one motif or another are rarely obvious on the finished quilted piece. What comes forth is the overall texture. So adjust as needed and keep on quilting!

As you grow in other skills, such as foresight and familiarity with design forms, you may need less flexibility. While you are still new to free-motion quilting, though, please be easygoing. Perfectionism has the terrible side effect of taking all the fun out of quilting.

Echoing

Echoing is common in quilting designs. The play of light and shadow in an echoed design has great visual impact. We'll use that to our benefit in a number of echoed designs. When echoing, keep a consistent space between the original line and the echoed line. A loose consistency is preferred over rigid precision; just do your best. As I've mentioned, when you step back from your quilting, small imperfections tend to disappear.

Foresight

One of the ways in which free-motion quilting challenges us is that we have to decide where to go next in our designs as we  cover the space to be quilted. Some designs make this easy. For instance, a line of loops goes in one direction. You make one initial direction decision and then just keep quilting in that direction. This makes designs with lines that go from one edge of the piece to the other attractive to new quilters: with fewer decisions to make, you can focus on the coordination aspect of free-motion quilting.

Some designs have a lot of possibilities. A basic pebbling design always has many options for where to place the next pebble. This makes it very accommodating. FIGURE A

Some designs have more limited possibilities. The fewer possible starting points for moving on to the next motif, the more attention you will need to pay to how you go about filling in your space.

The most challenging designs have even less flexibility. The motif has a set form, and wherever it ends is where you start the next motif. For these designs, a decision about which direction to take within the motif will affect where you find yourself once you've finished the motif. Thinking ahead to where you want to be when you've finished the current motif can help you work toward the areas you need to fill and avoid getting stuck in corners. Be aware of decision points in designs.

The decision point is mid design. The side you start the flower is the side you end the design.

The decision point is at the beginning. You end on the opposite side from the direction in which you begin drawing. As shown here, if you begin drawing toward the right, the design ends on the left.

Form Recognition

There are only so many ways to fit the same shapes together, and I bet that, flipping through this book, you've already noticed that some designs are similar to others. This is great! Because if you can see the similarities between two designs, you can use the familiarity you have with one design to help you quickly grow comfortable with a similar-but-not-the-same design. Designs that are formed similarly will fill in the space similarly. Not every design will fit easily into a category, but here are some basic forms to be familiar with.

NESTLED

Shapes squeeze together as close as possible, and each shape touches many others. The basic nestled design is pebbling. If you can cover space with pebbling, you should do fine with these designs: Ashore (page 74), Porthole (page 98), Diadem (page 132), Orbs (page 162).

Pebbling

Pebbling is simply stitching a bunch of circles nestled together.

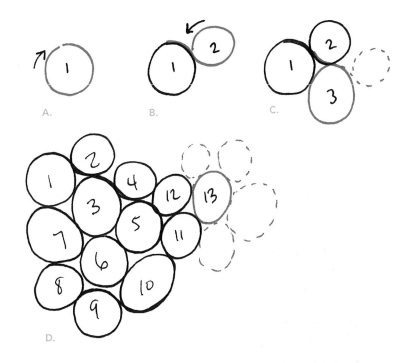

A. Form one circle.

B. Make another circle right beside it.

C. When you end between two pebbles, travel around a pebble along the line you've already made to reach an open space where you can start the next pebble.

D. Continue filling in the open space in this manner. Often you will have several spots available to place the next pebble.

BRANCHING

In these designs, a branch is formed, with extensions such as leaves or spirals to either side. When one branch is completed, the next branch is created, leading out from between extensions. If you understand the branching structure you can create many designs, including Trifles (page 78), Artemesia (page 118), Dainty (page 148), and Thicket (page 182).

EMERGING

In these designs, new motifs emerge from the space between two previously stitched motifs.

The basic emerging design is the paisley pattern. In these patterns, you will notice that empty areas form where three or four motifs meet. A few of my favorite emerging patterns are Flourish (page 42), Enchantment (page 48), Gilt (page 120), and Bower (page 174).

EDGE-TO-EDGE

Edge-to-edge designs are attractive to new machine quilters. Being able to work in one direction minimizes how often you need to rearrange the quilt and takes some of the pressure off of figuring out how to cover the space evenly. If the lines travel essentially straight you do need to be vigilant to keep them on course, but you won't have to work around getting stuck in a corner.

Something to keep in mind for edge-to-edge lines is that, for larger pieces, you may have to quilt half of the piece by stitching from one direction and the other half by stitching from the other direction (such as when you've turned your quilt upside down to stitch the left half from the left side without the rest of the quilt under the machine arm). If you will need to do this to quilt your piece, be sure to practice sketching and stitching your design in both directions before you start.

When quilting a horizontal edge-to-edge design, you may wish to orient the quilt sideways when you stitch, so that while the pattern is horizontal on the quilt, you are working vertically in relation to the machine. This will allow you to quilt with less bulk under your machine arm. Some of the most striking edge-to-edge designs in the book are Sylph (page 44), Adrift (page 70), Spindle (page 130), and Lumen (page 176).

BACK-AND-FORTH ECHOES

In these designs, the final step is echoing around previous shapes. Some designs echo a prescribed number of times, and you will need to think ahead to make sure you end up on the desired side of the design. Other designs can be echoed a variable number of times, or only echoed partially, allowing you to easily reach the point where you want to start the next motif. With echoing designs, be sure to leave room to echo back when you work near a tight space. If you have a preference for echoing designs, you should love these designs: Midsummer (page 64), Flora (page 138), Spectrum (page 146), and Verdure (page 154).

WANDERERS

In these designs, a motif is created and then joined to the next by another element, such as wavy or loopy lines. The connecting element may take any direction, and the design wanders across the open space. If you've had success with basic meandering quilting you will easily take to wandering designs, such as Bauble (page 46), Whistle (page 96), and Dizzy (page 110).

CLIMBERS

Some motifs "climb" by linking elements from bottom to top. You end each design element on top, leaving you ready to start the next one. These designs are flowing and flexible. Some climbing designs in this book are Haven (page 90), Bountiful (page 124), Traipse (page 136), and Rampant (page 170).

FROM A DESIGN YOU LIKE TO A FINISHED QUILT

So what do you do when you've found a design you like? Here's my prescription for getting to know it.

To start, read the instructions for forming the basic motif. Then look at the design sample to understand how the motifs work together to create the design. Once you are comfortable with the basic structure of the design, move on to sketching it.

Sketching lets you practice creating the design in empty space, making sure you understand the path the design takes. When you sketch, you practice the spacing, proportion, and rhythm of the design. You learn how to keep the design even and avoid working yourself into a corner. I don't think I can overstate the importance of taking time to sketch your design with pen and paper. It really pays off when you sit down in front of a project to quilt. You are already familiar with the design, and you haven't used any fabric or thread to gain that familiarity.

Most of the designs in this book did not come out right the first time I sketched them, but after filling a few pages I got the feel for them. If you're getting frustrated with a particular design, try this trick: Photocopy the design and then use a colored marker to follow the design as it's drawn. You'll gain muscle memory for the design while seeing how the design works across the open space. After doing this, try sketching on a blank page again.

Once you can fill an entire sheet of paper with your design, you are ready to practice it with needle and thread. Try at least a few minutes of practice stitching before jumping into a whole quilt. This will let you become comfortable with the quilting movements and allow you to check that you've chosen the right scale for quilting your design.

Now you're ready to quilt! If you go through the steps above I think you'll be pleased with what you see when you start quilting your piece.

The Designs

Cherish

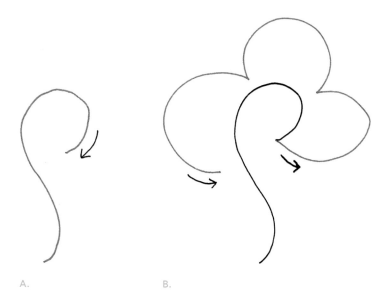

A.

B.

A. Make a loose spiral.

B. Draw 3 arcs around the outside. If you are not in a good place to start the next motif, echo around the outside of the arcs until you are.

Filament

A.

B.

C.

D.

A. Start with a row of evenly spaced arcs along the top edge of the piece.

B. Come back by extending into an arc and making a series of 3 loops.

C. Arc down and over to the middle of the adjacent arc and repeat all the way down the row.

D. Continue, with each row extending into the previous one.

Flitter

A.

B.

C.

A. Form a spiral; then travel back to its base.

B. Place a leaf around it.

C. Echo around the leaf; then start a new motif.

Mead

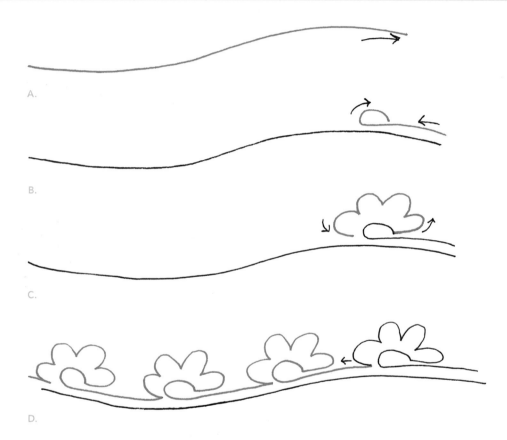

A. Start with a curving line.

B. Come back, echoing along the line, and then double back with an arc.

C. Add 4 arcs on the outside of the first arc.

D. Continue this pattern to make a chain of flowers down the line.

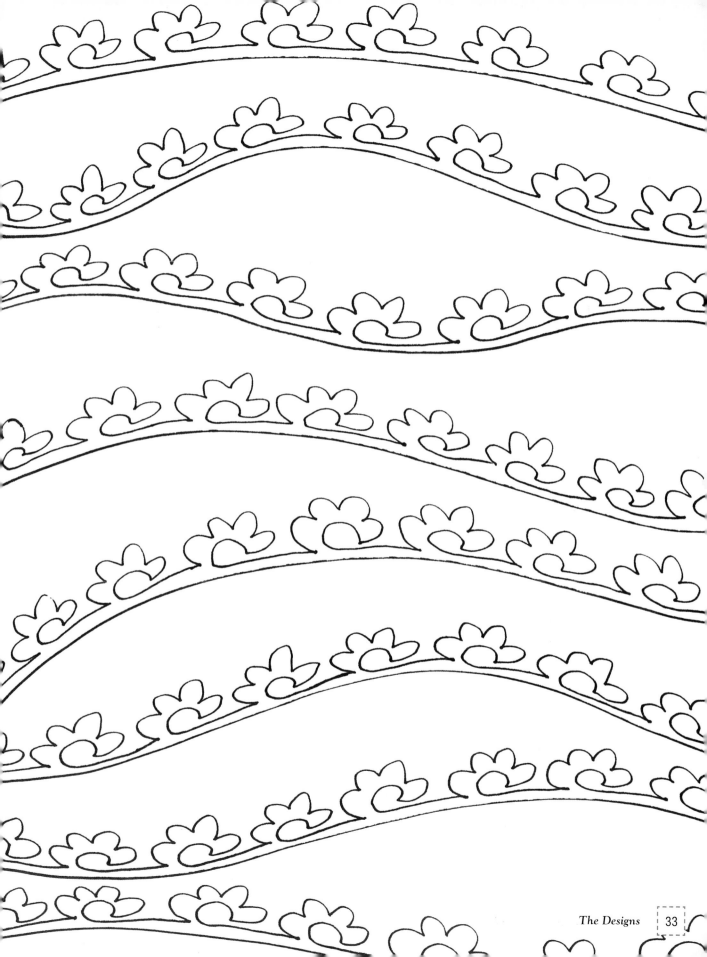

Unfurl

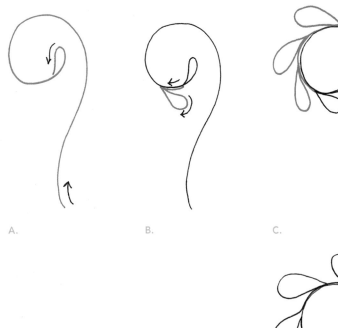

A. B. C.

D.

A. Make a spiral "stem" and end in a drop shape.

B. Travel a bit down the stem and add a slightly larger drop.

C. Continue with progressively larger drops until the stem is filled.

D. Travel back up the stem partway and start a new spiral stem.

Primordial

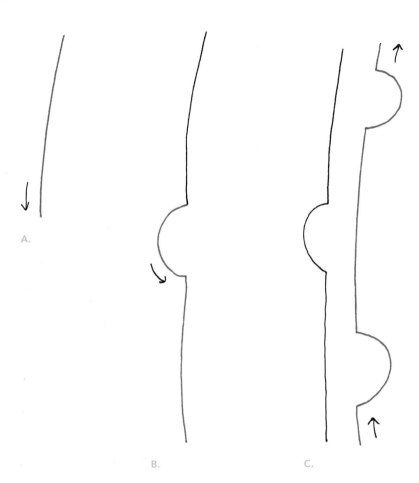

A. Start with a gently curving line.

B. Insert an arc and then continue the line. Insert more arcs down the length of the piece.

C. Come up by echoing the first line, inserting arcs offset from those on the first line.

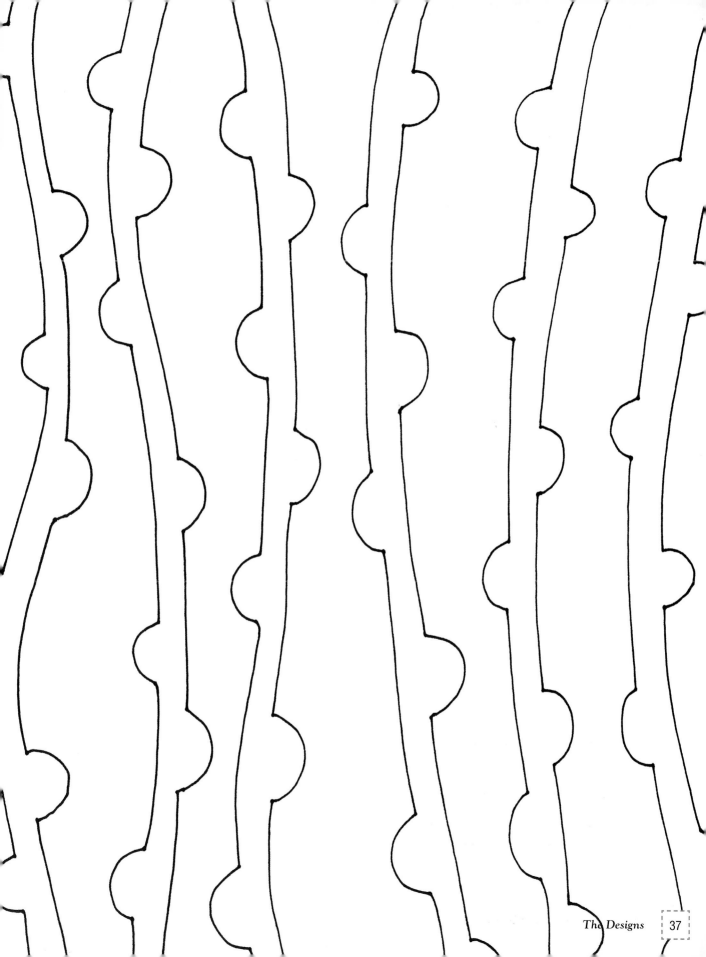

Sprig

A. Make a curving line ending in a drop shape.

B. Travel back down the line a bit and place a drop to one side.

C. Add a drop on the other side; then make more pairs of drops as you travel down the stem.

D. Echo around the drops.

E. Echo again until you get to the point at which you want to start the next motif.

Dimple

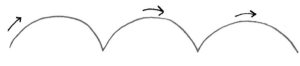

A.

B.

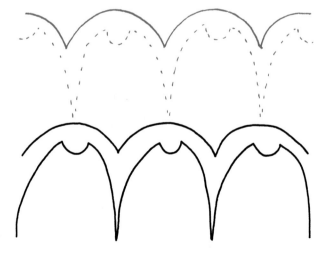

C.

A. Make a row of shallow arcs.

B. Come back, echoing along the underside of the arcs. Place a downturned arc at the top of each echo.

C. Start another row of shallow arcs.

Flourish

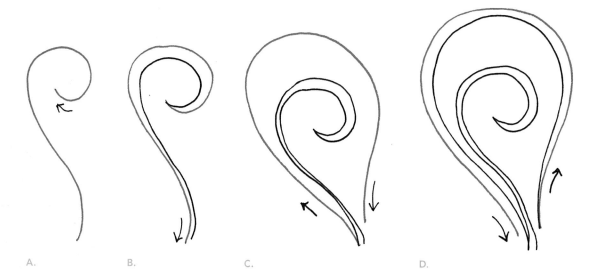

A.

B.

C.

D.

A. Make a long spiral.

- -

B. Come back out along the outside of the spiral.

- -

C. Make a drop shape around the spiral.

- -

D. Echo back around the drop once or twice; then start the next motif.

Sylph

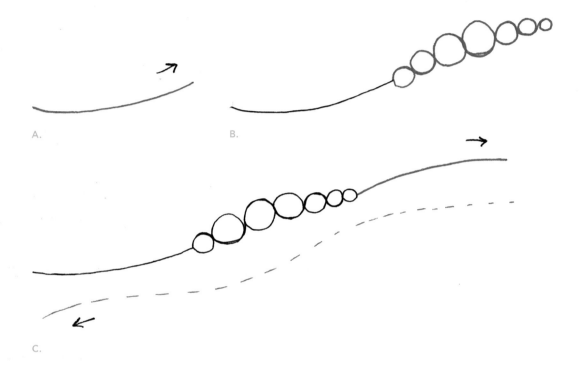

A. Start with a gently curving line.

B. Make a pebble line that continues the curve you started. Make the pebbles smaller at the ends and larger in the middle.

C. Continue the curving line. After each line with pebbles make a pebble-free line.

Bauble

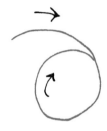  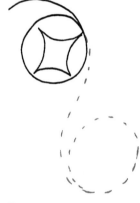

A.

B.

C.

A. Start with a curving line; then draw a circle.

B. Add a series of 4 arcs inside the circle.

C. Continue on with a curving line to the point at which you want to start the next motif.

Enchantment

A.

B.

C.

D.

A. Form a drop shape.

B. Fill the inside of the drop with a pebble line.

C. Travel back down the drop to its point and echo around the drop.

D. Echo one more time and start the next motif.

Espalier

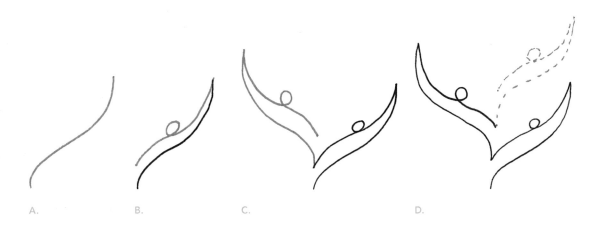

A.   B.   C.   D.

A. Start a gentle "S" curve at an angle.

B. Echo back along the top side of that curve, placing a loop halfway down.

C. Stop when you are above the point at which you started; then form the same motif toward the other side.

D. Continue upward in this manner, working from bottom to top.

Impulsive

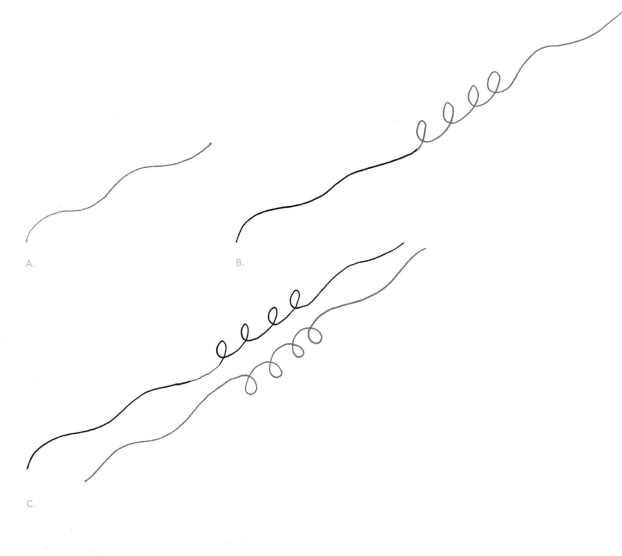

A. Create a curving line.

B. Add a series of 3 to 5 loops and continue the line. Add more series of loops as space allows.

- -

C. Come back in the opposite direction with another curving line. When you get to the loops on the adjacent line, mirror them.

Succulent

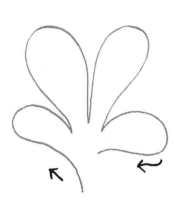 

A.

B.

A. Draw 4 open drop shapes to make a bloom.

B. Echo back around that bloom to the point at which you want to start a new motif. Depending on the space you have to fill, use more or fewer drops. Very tight areas may allow only one drop.

Happy Hour

A.

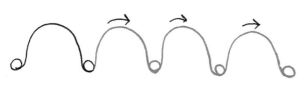

B.

C.

D.

E.

A. Start with a series of regularly spaced marks along the bottom edge of the piece.

B. Make a circle at the first mark.

C. Make an arc from there to the next mark and make another circle.

D. Continue down the length of the piece.

E. Come back in the opposite direction, offsetting each new row from the previous one.

Opulence

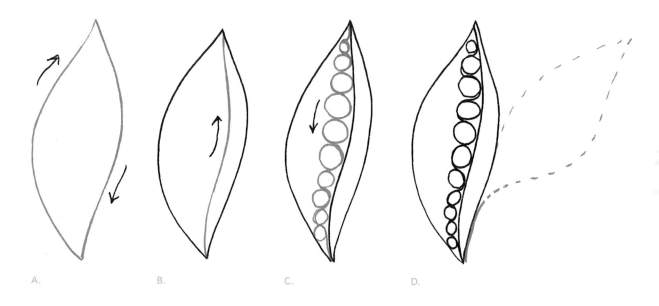

A. Start with a leaf shape.

B. Create a curving centerline.

C. Come down the centerline with a line of pebbles.

D. Travel up the leaf (if necessary) to where you want to start the next motif. Extend empty leaves into open spaces as needed.

Glimmer

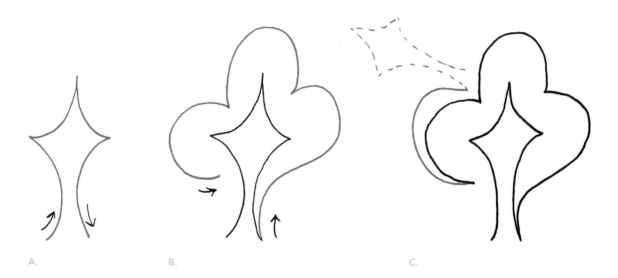

A.

B.

C.

A. Make a series of 4 arcs with their ends pointing outward.

B. Come back up and around, placing an arc over each point.

C. Echo around to the point at which you want to start the next motif.

Virtue

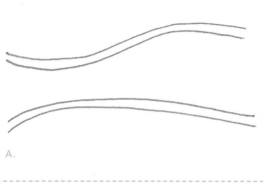

A.

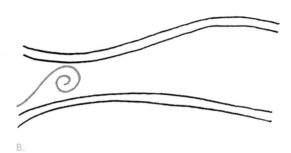

B.

C.

D.

A. Start with 2 sets of echoed curving lines.

B. Add a spiral between the curving lines. Leave some space to get out of the spiral.

C. Work back out of the spiral and directly into the next one.

D. Continue in this manner, changing the size of the spiral as needed to fill in the space.

Midsummer

A.

B.

C.

A. Start with an open circle.

- -

B. Place open leaf shapes around the circle.

- -

C. Echo back around to the point at which you want to start the next motif.

Bramble

 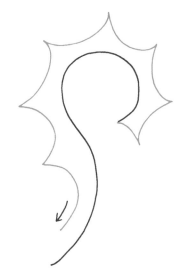 

A.   B.   C.

A. Make a loose spiral.

- -

B. Make a series of arcs around the outside, points outward.

- -

C. Echo back around the outside.

Lively

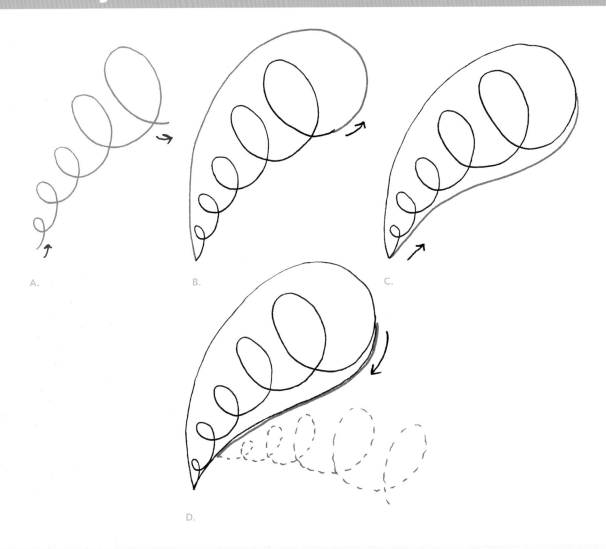

A. Make a series of successively larger loops.

B. Arc around the last loop back to your starting point.

C. Come back up the other side to complete a drop shape.

D. Travel around the outside to the point at which you want to start the next motif.

Adrift

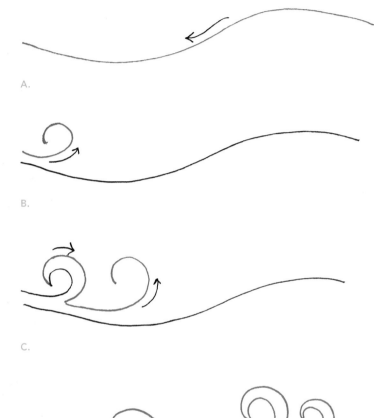

A.

B.

C.

D.

A. Start with a curving line.

B. Echoing just above the line, work back, inserting a loose spiral.

C. Echo along the outside of the spiral until you are even with the line. Draw another spiral.

D. Continue along the length of the line.

Breezy

A.

B.

C.

A. Make a loop.

B. Work around the loop with 4 arcs.

C. Echo around the outside of those arcs.

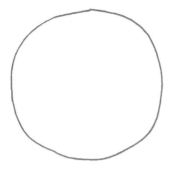

A.

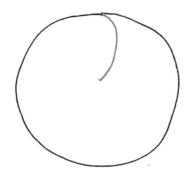

B.

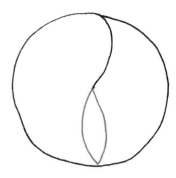

C.

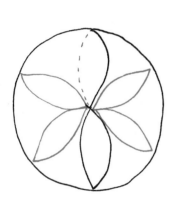

D.

E.

A. Form a circle.

B. Start a leaf that extends to the center of the circle.

C. Add a complete leaf below it.

D. Fill in 2 more leaves on each side; then complete the first leaf.

E. Place pebbles around the perimeter. Use pebbles to move outward to the point at which you want to start the next motif. Fill in open spaces with pebbles as you go.

Vestal

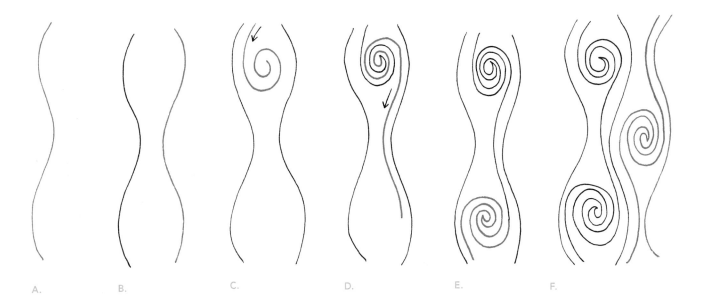

A.

B.

C.

D.

E.

F.

A. Start with a gentle "S" curve.

B. Mirror that curve.

C. Come down along one curve and insert a spiral into the open space between the lines.

D. Work back out of the spiral until you are beside the other curving line. Echo downward along that line to the next open space.

E. Insert another spiral and continue on down the column until it is filled.

F. Start a new mirroring "S" curve and continue on.

Trifles

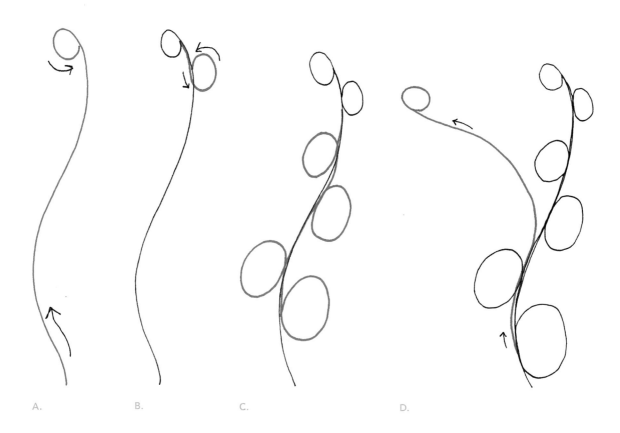

A.   B.   C.   D.

A. Start with a curving line and end with a circle.

B. Travel down the stem a little bit and add a circle on the other side.

- -

C. Continue down the stem, alternating sides, filling it with progressively larger circles.

D. Travel back up the stem to the point at which you want to start a new motif.

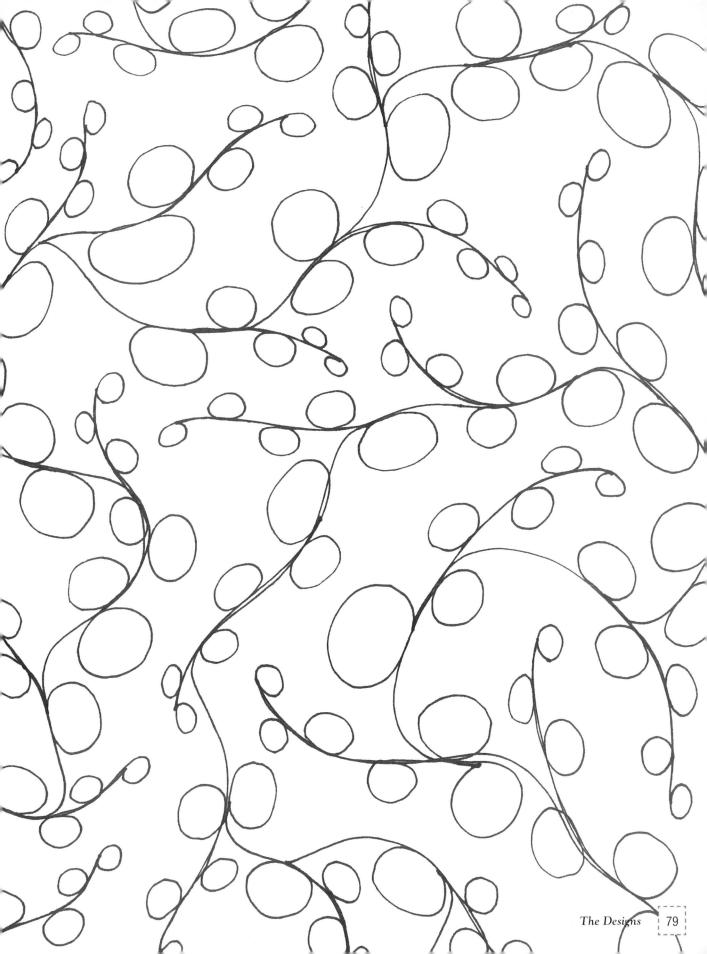

Mettle

A.

B.

C.

D.

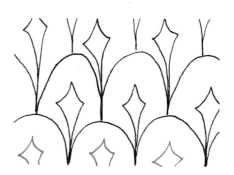

E.

F.

A. Start with a series of regular marks along the bottom edge of the piece.

B. Starting at one mark, make an elongated diamond from arc shapes, coming back to the mark.

C. Make an arc over to the next mark.

D. Repeat across the piece.

E. Work the next row back in the same manner, with diamonds and arcs, using the center of each arc below as your "mark."

F. When you've completed the quilting, come back and fill in with partial diamonds under the first row, if desired.

Winsome

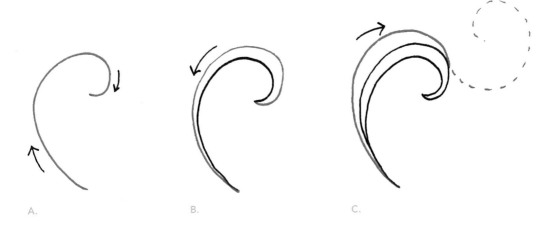

A. Start with a loose spiral.

- -

B. Echo back around the spiral to its starting point.

- -

C. Echo back up, bringing the echo to meet the previous line at the point at which you want the next motif to start.

Lithe

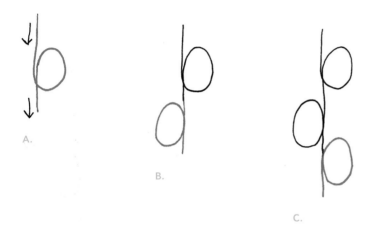

A.

B.

C.

A. Form a squat loop.

- -

B. Form another loop, extending in the opposite direction.

- -

C. Repeat all the way down the piece, letting the line gently drift right and left as you go.

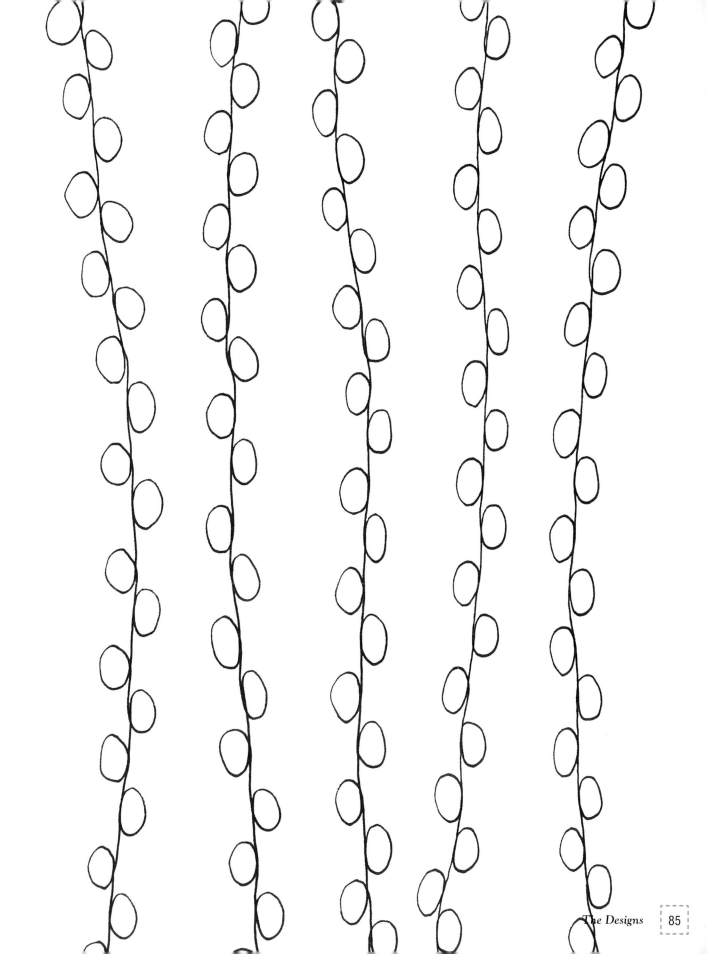

A. B. C.

D.

A. Form a spiral.

B. Place a row of arcs along the outside, crossing the spiral path when you come to it.

C. Add a revolution of open leaf shapes.

D. Place spirals around the flower until you are in a good place to start a new flower. Fill in with spirals as necessary.

Cadence

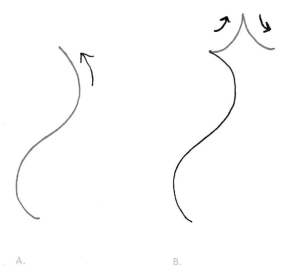

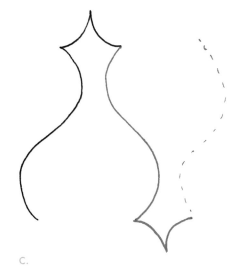

A.

B.

C.

A. Make an "S" curve. The top and bottom end-points should be roughly in line with each other.

- -

B. Add 2 arcs at the top, pointing up.

- -

C. Make a mirror curve down and add 2 arcs at the bottom. Repeat the pattern across the row.

Haven

A. B. C. D.

E.

A. Form an angled open leaf shape, starting with the top side.

B. Echo back around and stop when you are above the point where you started.

C. Repeat, making leaves on alternating sides.

D. Begin a bloom of 4 open drop shapes. Decision point: the side on which you start the bloom is the side where the next motif will start.

E. Echo back around the bloom and start a new motif.

Aspire

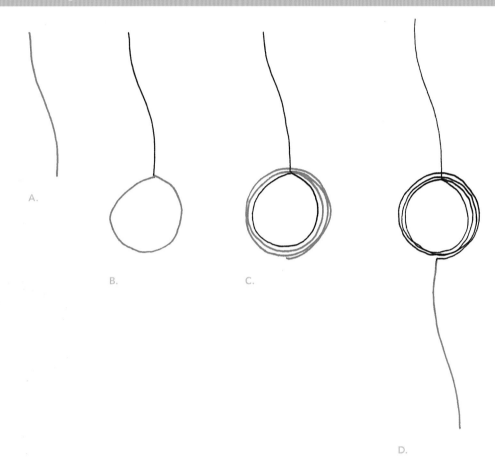

A.

B.

C.

D.

A. Start with a curving line.

B. Make a circle.

C. Echo tightly around the circle 2 or 3 times, ending at the bottom.

D. Continue the curving line, adding more circles as you go.

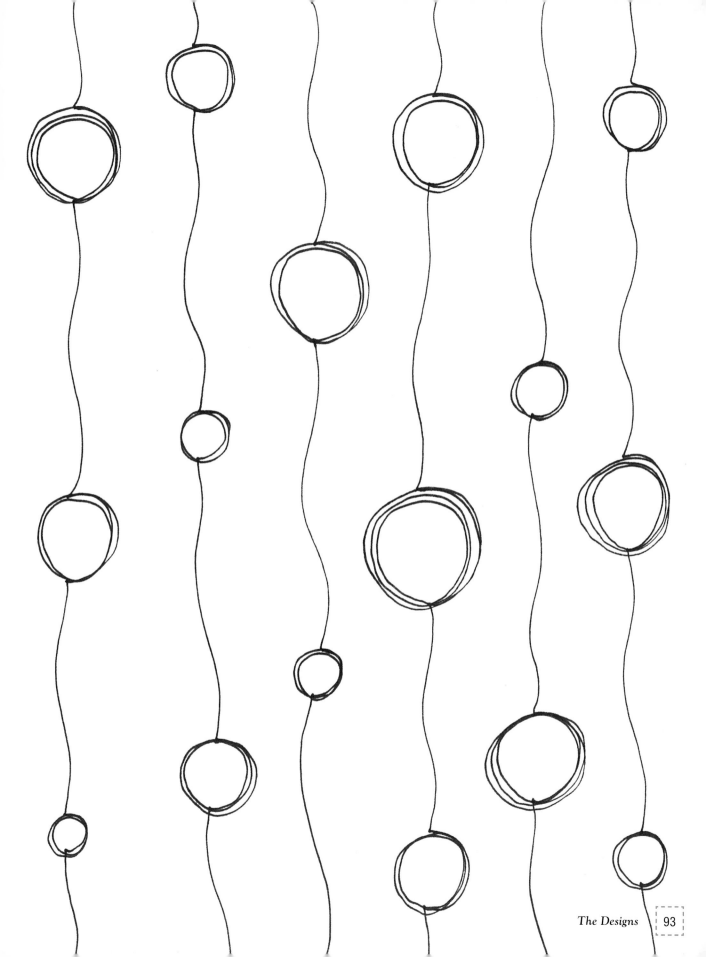

Tideway

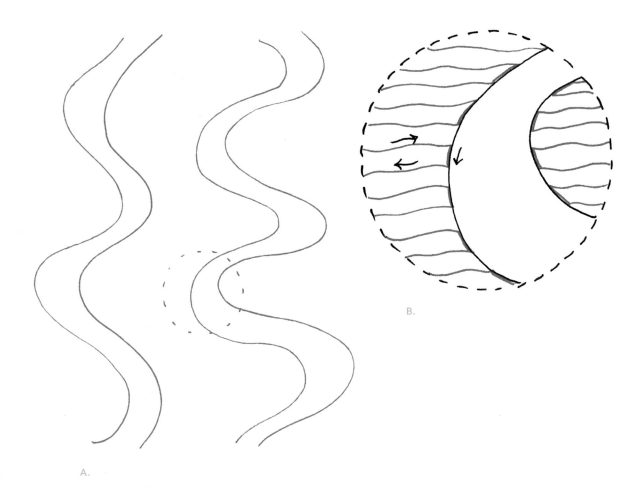

A.

B.

A. Start by making sets of curving lines from top to bottom across the piece.

B. Fill the space between the lines with close-set wavy horizontal lines. When a wavy line meets a curved line, travel along the curve to the point at which you want to start the next wavy line going back in the other direction.

Whistle

A.

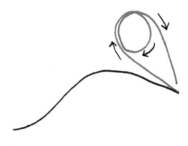

B.

C.

A. Make a curving line to the point where you want the center of your flower to be.

B. Start a drop shape, make a loop at the round end, and come back to the center.

C. Make 6 petals this way, ending in the center, and lead off with a new curving line.

Porthole

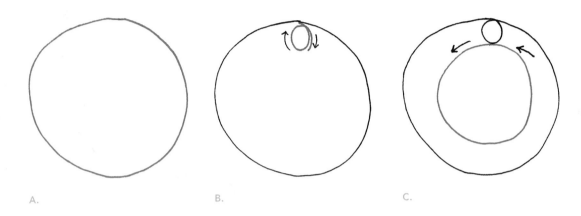

A.

B.

C.

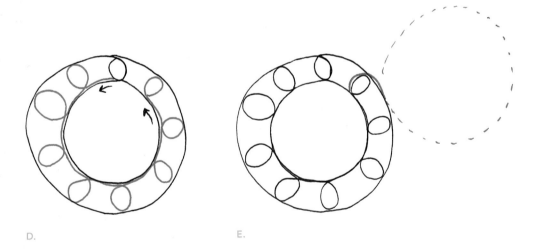

D.

E.

A. Make a large circle.

B. Make a loop inside the circle.

C. Travel to the other side of the loop and make a new circle in the center of the first.

D. Travel along the inner circle, making a series of loops all the way around.

E. Travel back to the outside circle and around to the point at which you want to start a new circle.

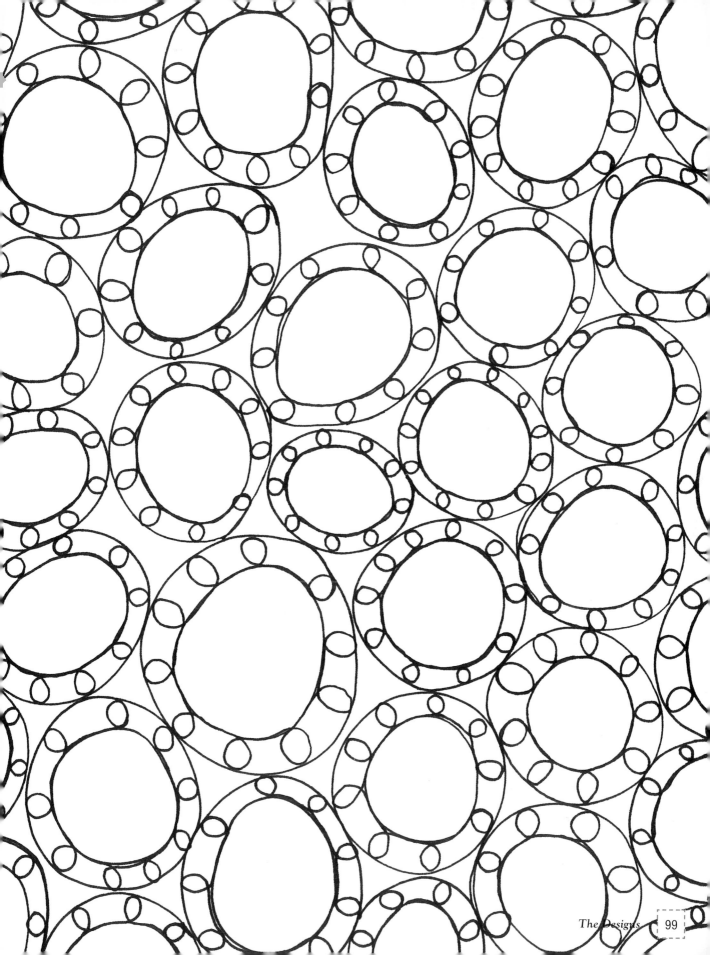

Wisp

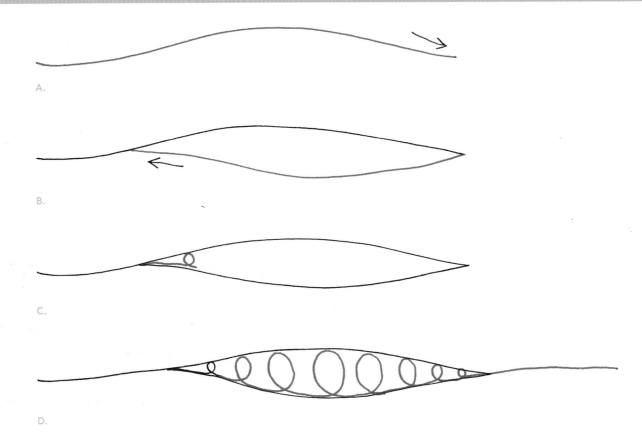

A.

B.

C.

D.

A. Start with a curving line.

B. Arc back to the line, forming a leaf shape.

C. Travel up one side of the leaf and extend a loop to touch the other side.

D. Fill the leaf shape with spaced loops; then travel to the point of the leaf and continue on with the line, adding more leaves as you go.

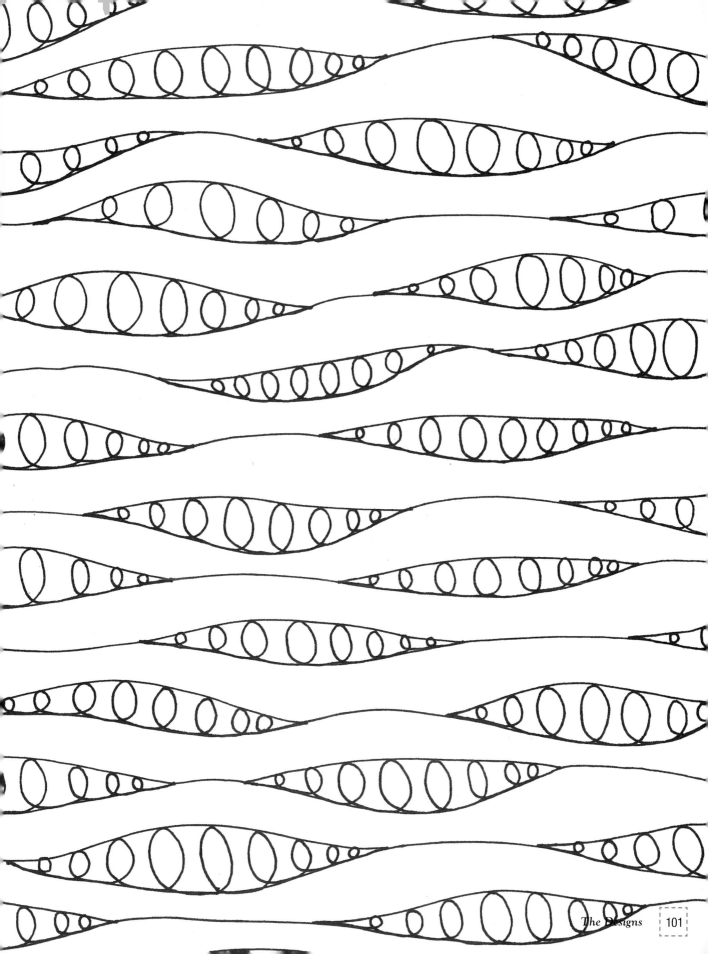

Billow

A. Start with a gentle "S" curve.

B. Come up, echoing along that curve and extending open drop shapes to the side.

- -

C. Make a mirror "S" curve and come up the opposite side of it with drop shapes.

D. Make the next "S" curve loosely follow the nearest one. This offsets the columns so they fit together nicely.

Lighthearted

A. Start with a looping line. Stop where you want the center of your flower to be.

B. Make a flower from 5 or 6 drop shapes.

C. Echo around the flower, ending in the center, and then lead off with a new loopy line.

Valiant

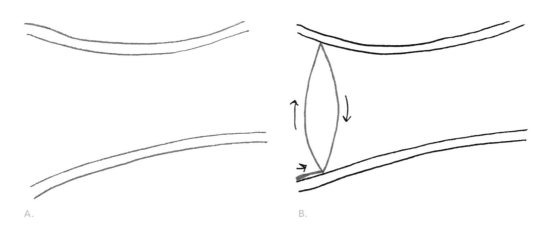

A.

B.

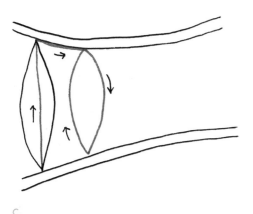

C.

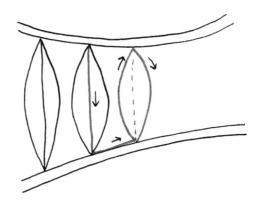

D.

A. Form 2 sets of echoed curving lines.

B. Travel along the bottom inner line. Form a leaf that touches the inner lines at its points.

C. Come up the center of the leaf; then travel along the upper line until you get to the point at which you want to place the next leaf.

D. Make the centerline of that leaf downward, and continue on in this manner.

Fervent

A.

B.

C.

A. Start a loop but don't close it.

B. Add 3 arcs around the loop.

C. Add a series of open leaves. If you are not in a good
place to start the next motif, echo around until you are.

Step-by-Step Free-Motion Quilting

Dizzy

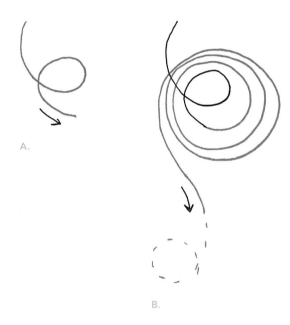

A.

B.

A. Make a loop.

B. Echo outward in a tight spiral 3 or 4 times; then start a new loop.

Grove

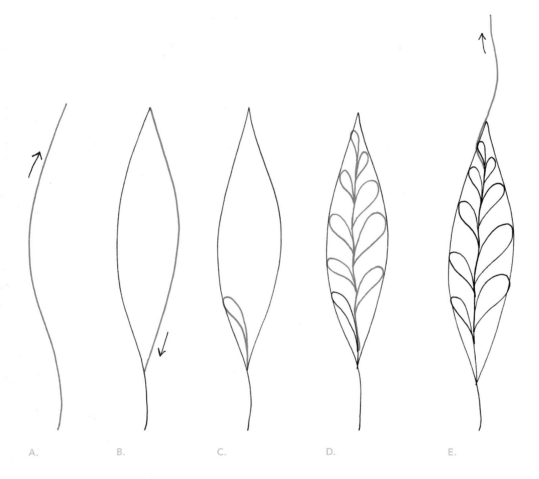

A. Make a curving line.

B. Arc back down to the line to make a leaf shape.

C. Extend a drop shape to one side.

D. Fill up the shape with alternating drops.

E. Travel back up to the top point of the leaf. Continue on with the line, adding more leaves as you go.

Fandangle

A.   B.   C.

D.

A. Make an arc.

B. Extend a spiral under the arc and return to the end of the arc.

C. Continue down the row.

D. Return in the opposite direction, offsetting the arcs from row to row.

Swift

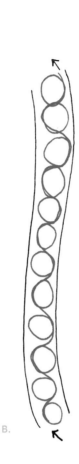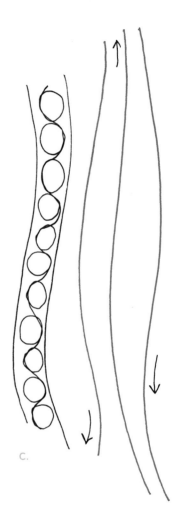

A.

B.

C.

A. Create a set of echoed curving lines.

- -

B. Place a line of pebbles between the curving lines.

- -

C. Make a series of 3 or 4 more curving lines with no pebbles between them; then repeat the pattern from the beginning.

Artemesia

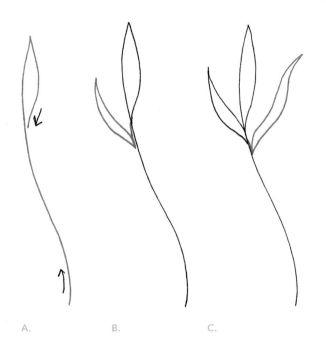

A. B. C.

A. Start with a curving line and end with a grass shape.

- -

B. Travel a bit down the line and add a grass shape on one side.

- -

C. Travel down a bit more and add a grass shape on the other side.

- -

D. Continue this way until the stem is full.

- -

E. Travel back up the stem to the point at which you want to start the next motif.

D. E.

Gilt

A.   B.   C.

A. Begin a drop shape but arc into its center halfway up. You may start at either side of the drop shape, depending on where you want the arc to be. The design works best when you irregularly alternate between starting at the left and starting at the right of the motif.

- -

B. Echo back along the top of the arc and complete the drop shape.

- -

C. Echo around the outside and start the next motif.

Stellate

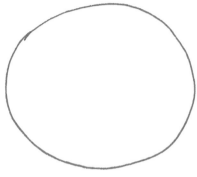

A.

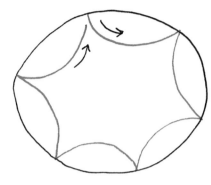

B.

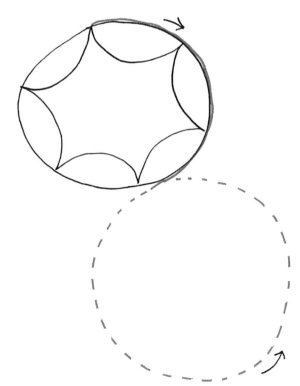

C.

A. Make a large circle.

B. Place a series of arcs inside.

C. Travel around the circle to the point at which you want to start the next circle.

Bountiful

A. Form an angled open drop shape, starting with the top edge.

B. Echo back around until you are above your starting point.

C. Repeat, making drops to alternating sides.

D. To start a bloom, create a grass shape. Decision point: Come down on the side on which you want the next motif to start.

E. Make an open leaf and echo it.

F. Move around the leaf with arcs and echo back; then start the next motif.

Rapunzel

A. Create a curving line and insert a spiral.

- -

B. Travel back along the spiral to the point at which you can continue the line. Make a new spiral in the opposite direction. Repeat all the way up the piece.

- -

C. Come down from the opposite direction with a new line of spirals. Where a line passes a spiral loop (noted with ✳ on the illustration), the line should touch the spiral.

A.   B.   C.

Lilypad

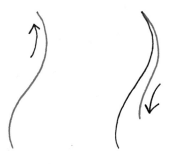

A.   B.

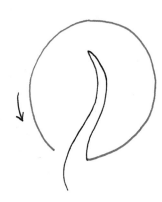 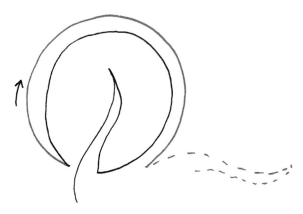

C.   D.

A. Start a grass shape.

B. Decision point: the side you come down on is the side on which you will start the next motif.

C. Make an open circle around the grass shape.

D. Echo back around the outside; then start the next motif.

Spindle

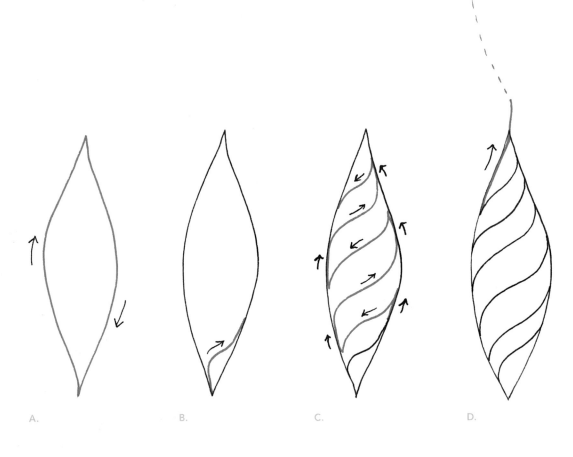

A. Make a leaf.

B. Travel up the edge a bit and make a loose "S" shape inside the leaf.

C. Travel up the other side a bit and come down with another "S" shape. Continue up the leaf in this manner until it is filled.

D. Travel along the edge to the tip; then continue up a bit to start the next motif.

Diadem

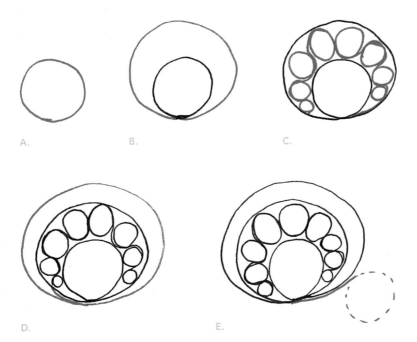

A.

B.

C.

D.

E.

A. Make a circle.

B. Echo around that circle.

C. Fill in the space between the circles with a line of pebbles.

D. Echo around one more time.

E. Travel around the outer circle to the point at which you want to start the next motif.

Muse

A.

B.

C.

A. Start by joining 4 open drop shapes.

B. Work around the drop shapes with open leaves.

C. Echo back around the leaves; then use spirals around the perimeter and to fill in empty space until you reach the point at which you want to start the next motif.

Traipse

A. Start an angled open leaf shape, beginning with the top edge, and end in a spiral.

B. Echo around the outside of this shape until you are above the point at which you started.

C. Form another leaf angled toward the other side, without the spiral.

D. Continue up in this manner. Add a spiral leaf every third leaf or so.

E. Form an open circle. Decision point: if you want to start the next motif on the right, start the circle to the left (draw it clockwise), and vice versa.

F. Echo around the circle twice and start the next motif.

Flora

A.   B.   C.   D.

A. Form a spiral.

- -

B. Come back out on the inside of the spiral.

- -

C. Create 5 petals with arcs.

- -

D. Echo the arcs until you get to the point at which you want to start a new motif.

Leafy

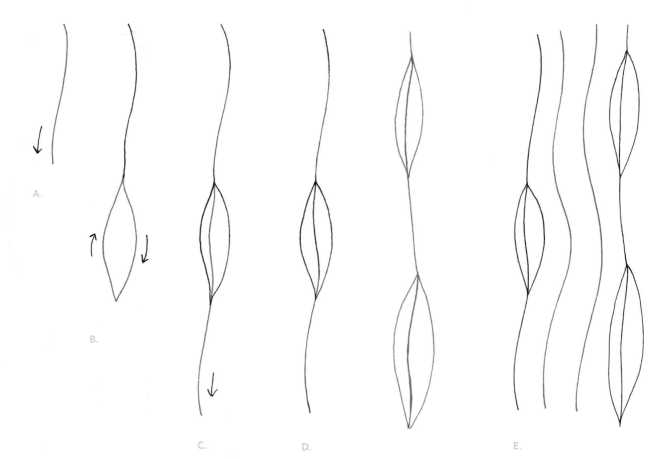

A. Start with a gently curving line.

B. Make a leaf shape.

C. Continue the line down through the leaf, adding more leaves as you go.

D. Make more lines, staggering the leaves.

E. Add gently curving lines without leaves between the lines with leaves, echoing the adjacent lines loosely.

Pop

A. Make a spiral and echo around the outside.

B. Add 2 arcs.

C. Make a small spiral and come back on the outside. Start a new motif or echo around to the point at which you want to start a new one.

Temperance

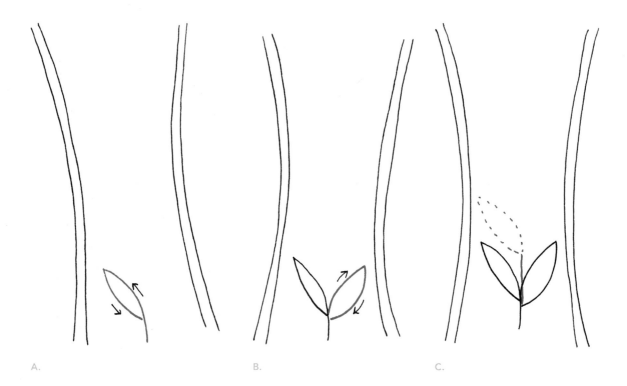

A. Start with 2 sets of echoed curving lines. Starting at the bottom, come up between the lines with a curving line. Extend a leaf to one side.

B. Draw a leaf to the other side.

C. Move up a bit and start another set of leaves. Continue upward in this manner.

Spectrum

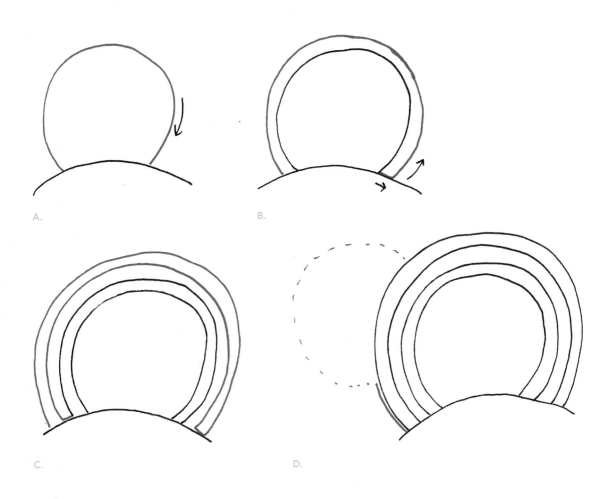

A. Make a partial circle. The base of the circle should be a circle you've already stitched or the edge of the piece.

B. Travel to the side along the base and echo around the original circle.

C. Continue traveling to the side and echoing until you have 4–6 circles.

D. Travel up the outermost echo to the point at which you want to start the next motif.

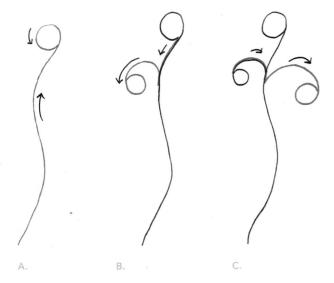

A.

B.

C.

D.

E.

A. Start with a curving line and end in a circle.

B. Travel back down the line; then make an arc to the side and end in a circle.

C. Travel back along the arc to the stem; then make another arc ending in a circle to the other side.

D. Continue down the stem in this manner until you've filled its open space.

E. Travel back up the stem to the point at which you want to start the next motif.

Ablaze

A. Make a curving line from top to bottom.

B. Come back along the line with open grass shapes.

C. Make another line nearby. Come back with grass shapes on the opposite side.

Precious

A. Start a drop shape. At the curved end of the drop, make a loop.

B. Complete the drop.

C. Echo the drop 2 times.

D. Start a new motif.

E. When an empty triangle forms between motifs, fill it with pebbles.

Verdure

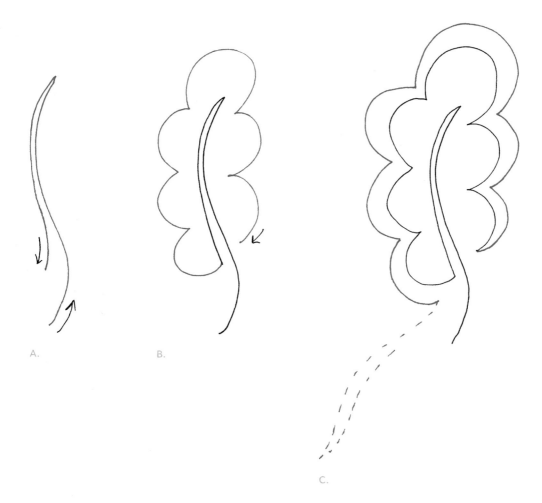

A.

B.

C.

A. Make a grass shape.

B. Work up one side and down the other with arcs.

C. Echo back around the arcs until you are in the right place to start the next motif.

Bangle

 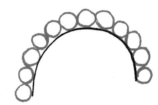 

A.

B.

C.

A. Start with an arc.

- -

B. Place a line of pebbles on the outside.

- -

C. Travel back along the arc to the point at which you want to start the next motif.

Pragma

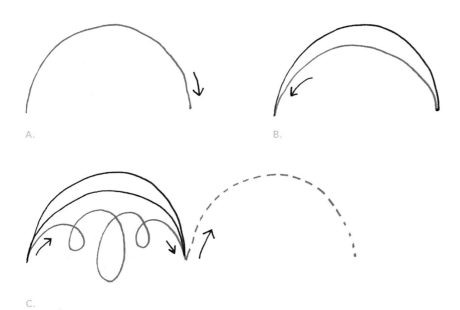

A.

B.

C.

A. Start with an arc.

B. Echo back on the underside of the arc.

C. Make a series of 3 loops under the arc, with the middle one longest; then start another arc.

Build successive rows upward, offsetting each row by half an arc.

Rugged

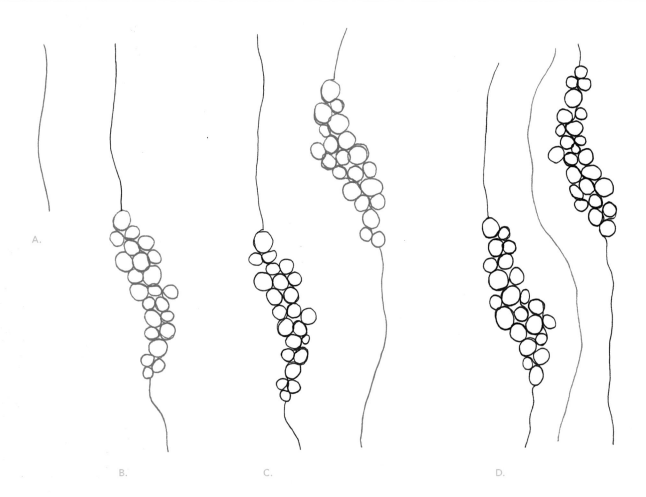

A. Start with a curving line.

B. Make an irregular skinny cluster of pebbles; then continue the curving line. Add more pebble clusters as you go. Keep the lines unpredictable, with a random wavy appearance.

C. Make more lines, varying the placement of the clusters.

D. Insert more curving lines without pebble clusters between the lines with clusters.

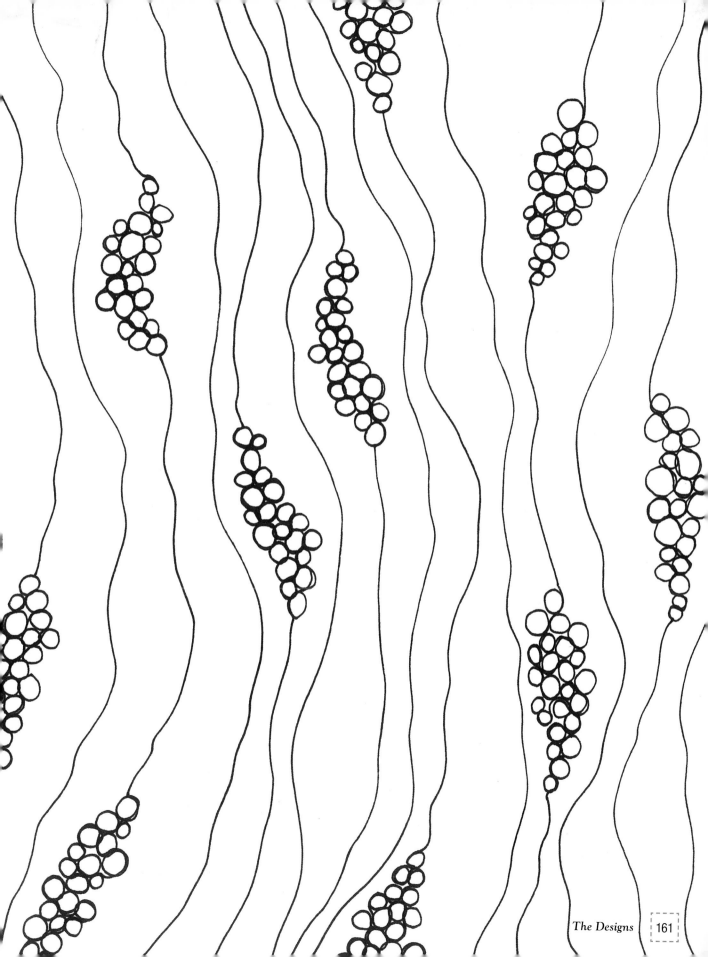

Orbs

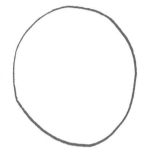  

A.   B.   C.

D.

A. Form a circle.

B. Arc toward the circle's middle and echo back to the circle.

C. Travel around the circle and make another arc.

D. Add more arcs until the circle is filled and then begin the next motif.

Effervescent

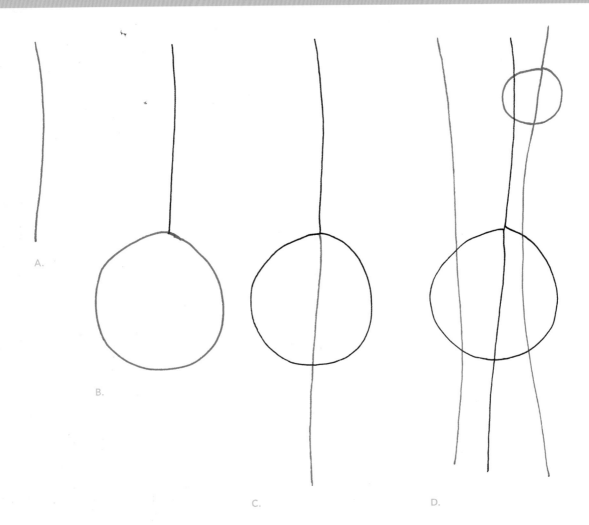

A. Start with a gently curving line.

B. Make a circle.

- -

C. Continue the curving line through the circle.

D. Make more lines with circles of varying sizes. Let the lines and circles overlap.

Cumulus

A. Start with a curving line.

- -

B. Create an irregular cluster of spirals and then continue the curving line. Add more clusters as you go.

- -

C. Echo along the top and bottom of each line.

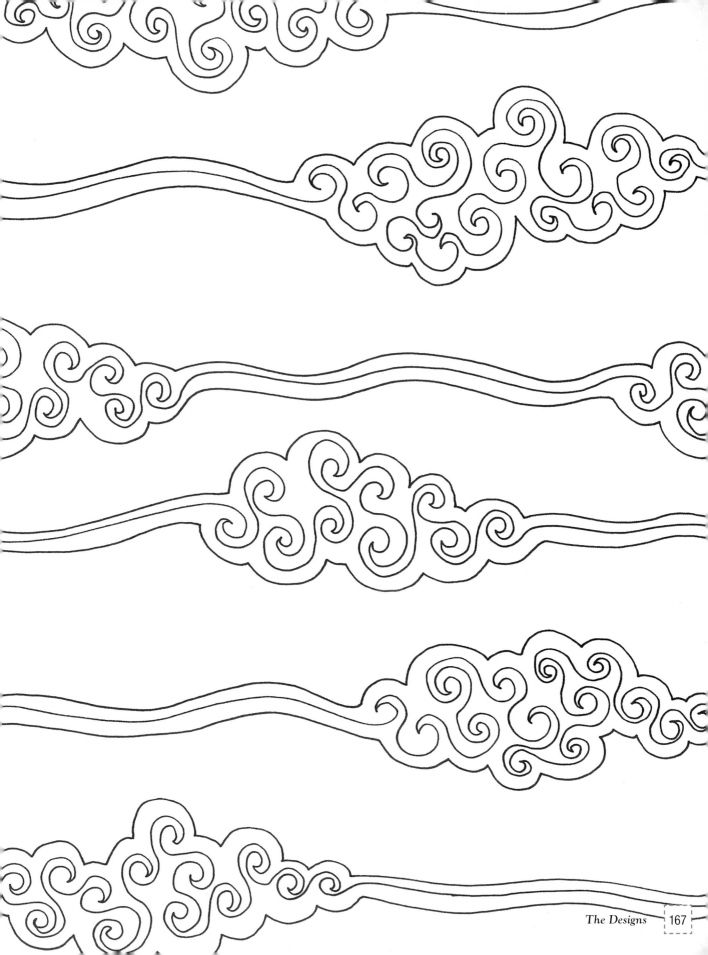

Gossamer

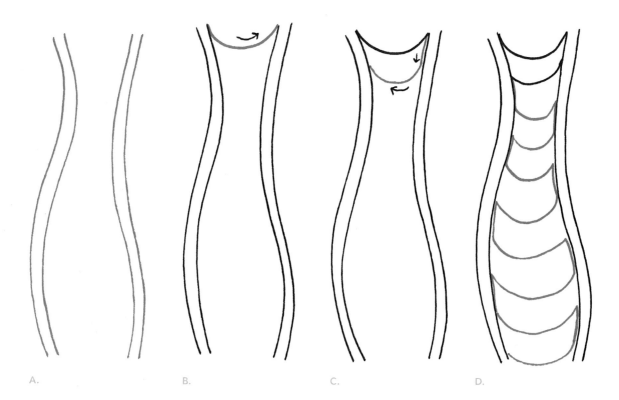

A. Start with 2 sets of echoed curving lines.

B. Draw an arc between the inner lines.

C. Travel down an inner line a bit; then make another arc.

D. Fill the whole column in this manner.

Rampant

A. Start a spiral.

B. Come back along the outside, ending above where you started.

C. Make more spirals to either side.

D. Begin a bloom from 3 open leaf shapes. Decision point: the side you start on is the side on which you will start the next motif.

E. Echo back around the bloom; then start a new motif.

A.

B.

C.

D.

E.

Garland

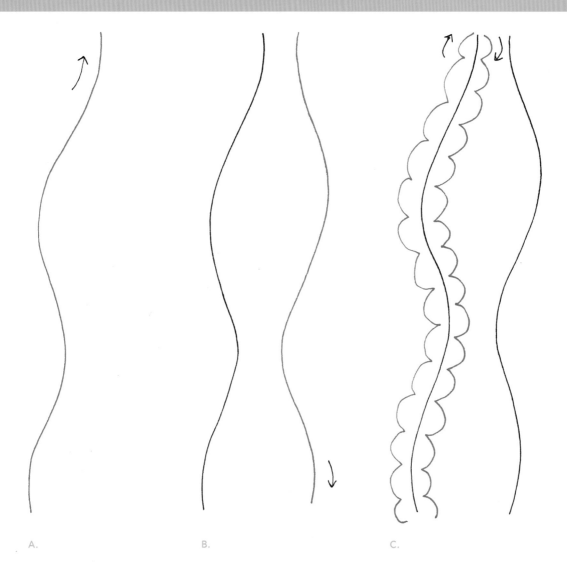

A. Make an "S" curve.

B. Make a mirror to that line. Do not let the lines get too close.

C. Echo up one side of one curve with a series of arcs and then echo back down the other side. Repeat with the mirror curve.

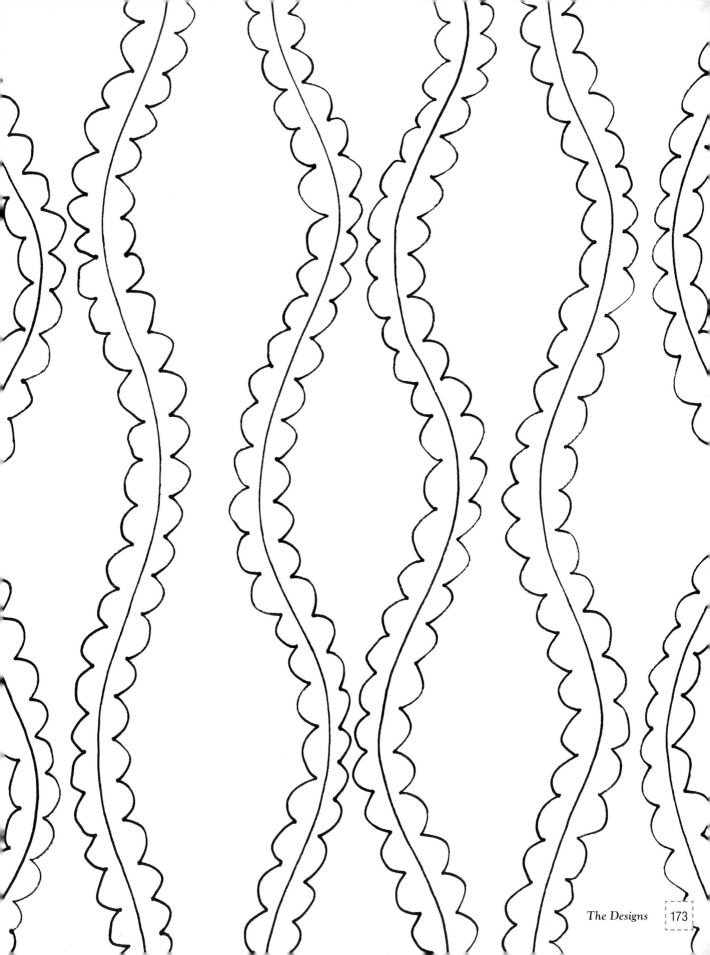

Bower

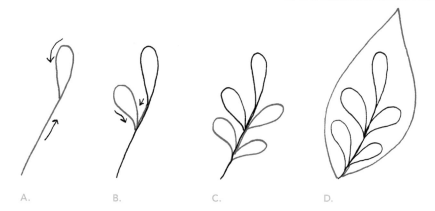

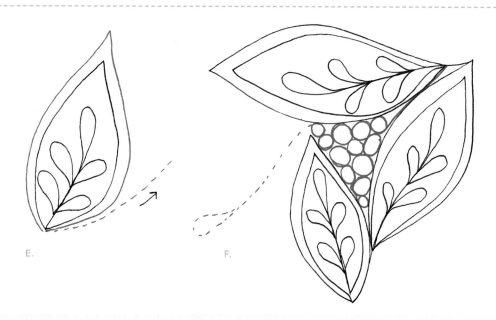

A. Form a stem with a drop end.

B. Travel down the stem a short way and add a drop.

C. Add a drop to the other side and then make another set of drops lower.

D. Make a leaf shape around the stem and drops.

E. Echo around the leaf shape and then start a new motif.

F. Where an open space is formed between leaves, travel into the area and fill it with pebbles; then continue on with the design.

Lumen

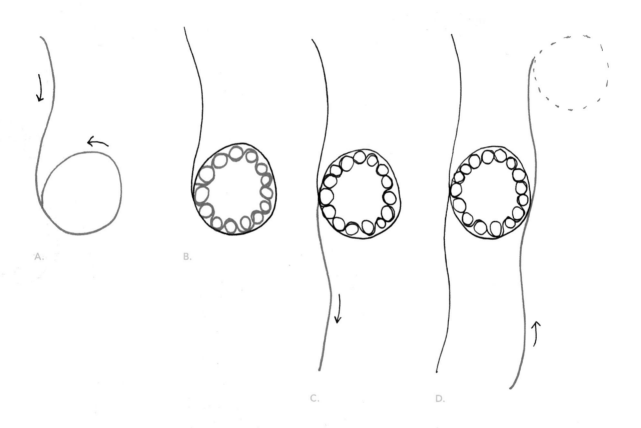

A. Start with a curving line. Extend a large circle to one side.

B. Traveling along the inside of the circle, create a line of pebbles.

C. Continue the curving line, adding more circles as you go.

D. Begin another curving line. Make sure the lines touch the edges of the circles as they pass.

Frills

A.

B.

C.

A. Make a spiral.

- -

B. Place a series of arcs along the outside of the spiral.

- -

C. Come back up, echoing the arcs, to the point at which you want to start the next motif.

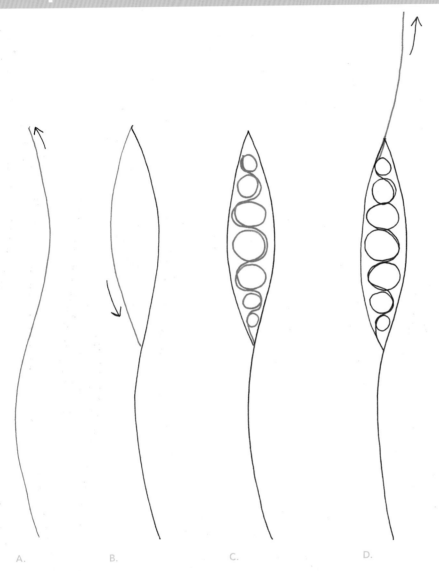

A. Start with a curved line.

B. Arc back down to meet the line, making a leaf shape.

C. Fill in the shape with a line of pebbles.

D. Travel to the point of the leaf and continue on in the original direction. Add more leaves periodically. Stagger the placement of leaves from one adjacent line to the next.

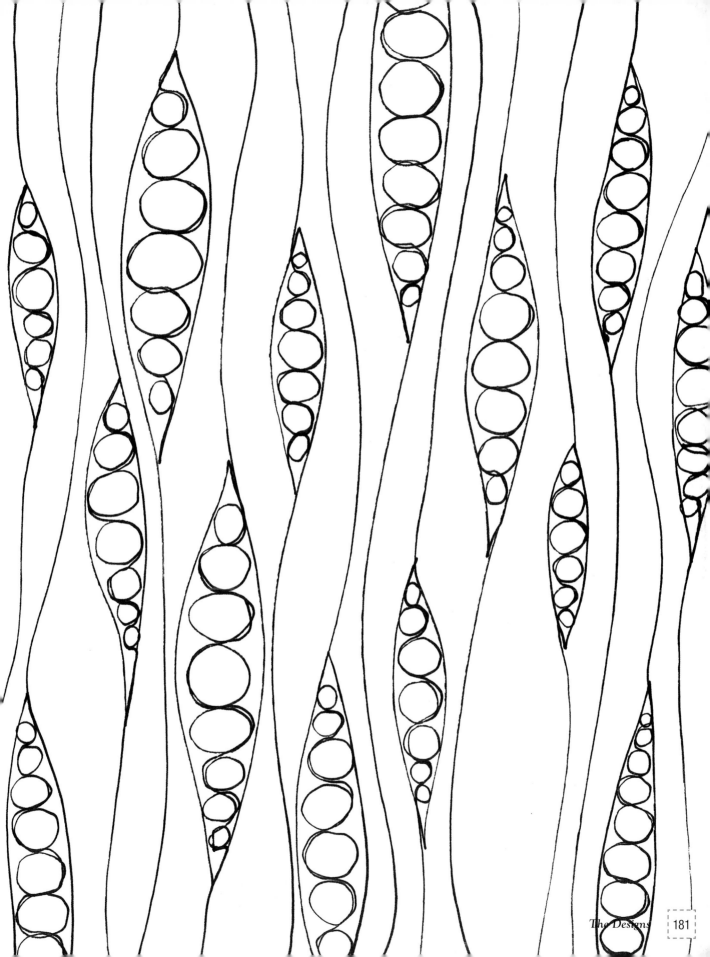

Thicket

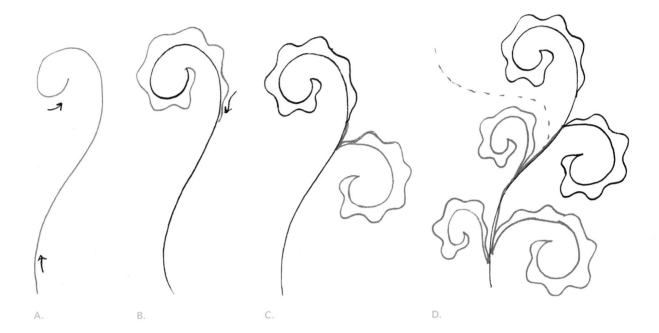

A. Start with a curving line that ends in a spiral.

B. Echo around the spiral with an "S" curve and come back to the curving line.

C. Travel down the line a bit and form a similar spiral with an "S" curve echo to the side.

D. Add spirals down the line; then travel back up the line to the point at which you want to start the next motif.

Enoki

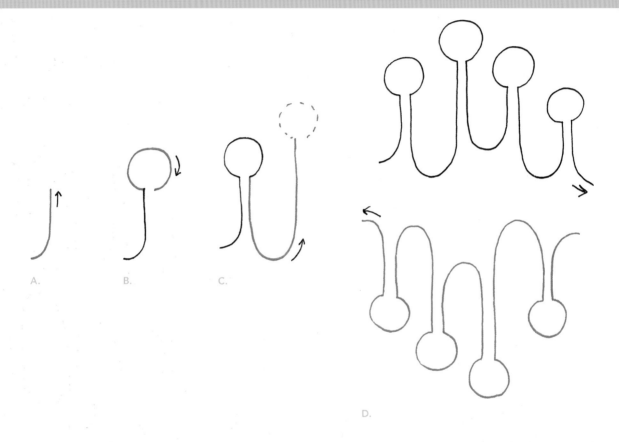

A. Start at one edge of the piece with half an arc.

B. Add an open circle at the end.

C. Make another arc and continue making arcs and circles down the line, varying the heights.

D. Come back in the same manner, making the motifs in the opposite direction.

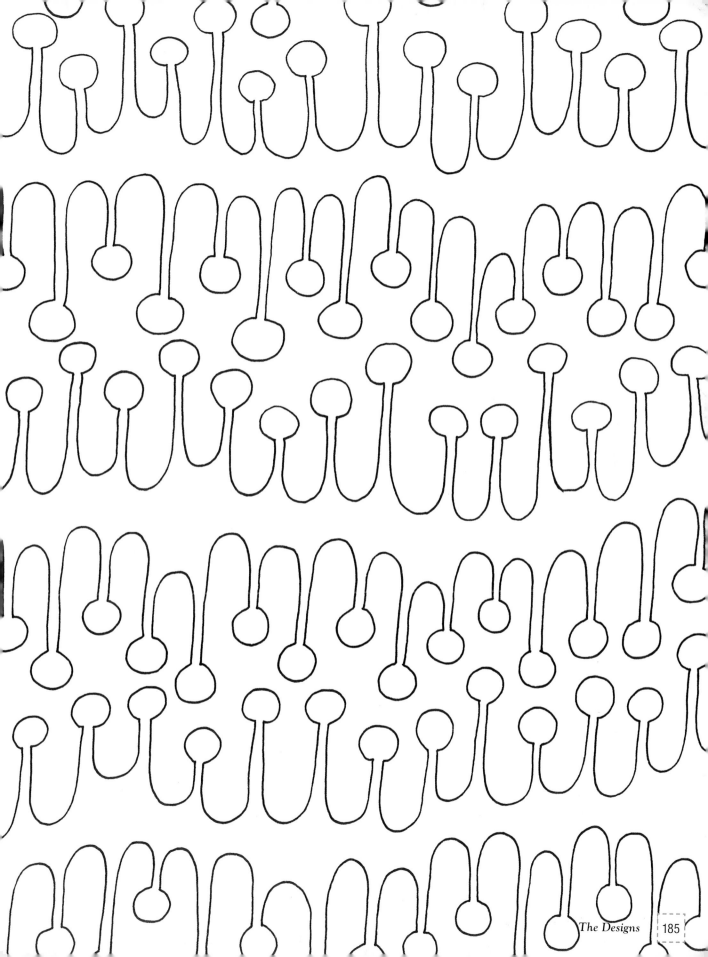

Lather

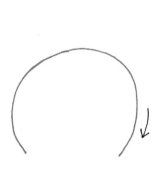

A.

B.

C.

A. Make a large arc.

- -

B. Come back with a series of small arcs around the outside.

- -

C. Come back with 1–2 more layers of arcs until you are in the right place to start the next motif.

Ripple

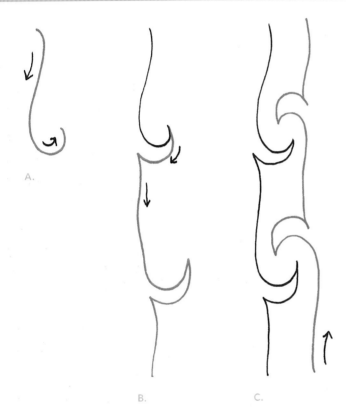

A.

B.   C.

A. Start with a curving line and arc out to the side.

B. Echo back and continue the line. Add more arcs as you go.

C. Come back up, making arcs that curve to fit the arcs of the adjacent line.

Afterword

This book only scratches the surface of what is possible when you put simple shapes together. So many more designs are out there.

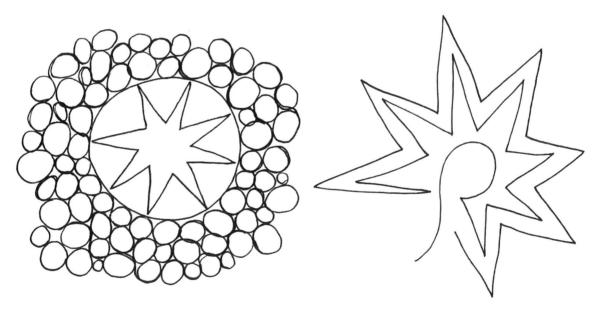

Take a moment to look closely at the quilting designs that you see out in the world. Break them down into their motifs and then break the motifs down into the basic shapes that create them. I wish you well on your quilting romps. Keep dreaming up new ideas, trying new things, and having fun!

About the Author

Photo by Jill Browning

CHRISTINA CAMELI is a nurse-midwife and quilter who enjoys finishing quilts on her domestic machine in addition to teaching free-motion quilting classes for beginners. She is the author of *First Steps to Free-Motion Quilting* and lives in Portland, Oregon.

ALSO BY CHRISTINA CAMELI:

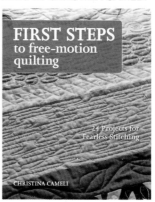

stash BOOKS

fabric arts for a handmade lifestyle

ctpub.com